Animal Lives
EAGLES

Sally Morgan

QEB Publishing, Inc.

Copyright © QEB Publishing, Inc. 2005

Published in the United States by
QEB Publishing, Inc.
23062 La Cadena Drive
Laguna Hills, CA 92653

www.qeb-publishing.com
Reprinted in 2007

All rights reserved. No part of this publication
may be reproduced, stored in a retrieval
system, or transmitted in any form or
by any means, electronic, mechanical,
photocopying, recording, or otherwise,
without the prior permission of the publisher,
nor be otherwise circulated in any form of
binding or cover other than that in which it
is published and without a similar condition
being imposed on the subsequent purchaser.

Library of Congress Control Number:
2005921283

ISBN 978 1 59566 497 6

Written by Sally Morgan
Designed by Q2A Solutions
Editor Tom Jackson
Map by PCGraphics (UK) Ltd

Publisher Steve Evans
Creative Director Louise Morley
Editorial Manager Jean Coppendale

Printed and bound in China

Picture credits

Corbis: Front Cover W Perry Conway,
George D Lepp 5, Eric and David Hosking
7, Bettmann 10, Ron Sanford 11, W Perry
Conway 13, 23, Joe McDonald 16, Philip
Richardson/Gallo Images 18, Uwe Walz 20,
Mary Ann McDonald 24, Galen Rowell 29
Ecoscene: Fritz Polking 14, Peter Cairns 24
FLPA: Jurgen & Christine Sohns 1, Winfried
Wisniewski 4, 6, 7, Michael Callan 12, Tom
and Pam Gardner 21, KLAUS NIGGE/FOTO
NATURA 22
Getty Images: Grant Faint/The Image Bank
8–9, Art Wolfe 15, 30, John Warden/Stone 25,
Joseph Van Os/The Image Bank 27
Still Pictures: Fritz Polking 17, Gunter Ziesler
19, JEREMY WOODHOUSE/WWI 23, DANIEL
DANCER 28, Clyde H Smith 30, Thomas D
Mangelsen 30

Title page: Bald eagle

Words in **bold** are
explained in the
Glossary on page 31.

Contents

Eagles 4

Eagle types 6

Where do you find eagles? 8

Building a nest 10

Laying eggs 12

Growing up 14

Flying 16

Eagle senses 18

Feeding 20

Hunting 22

Territories 24

Eagle communication 26

Eagles under threat 28

Life cycle 30

Glossary 31

Index 32

Eagles

Eagles are among the largest and most powerful of all birds. They are **birds of prey**—large birds that hunt other animals for food. To help them hunt, eagles have a powerful hooked beak, excellent eyesight, and feet that end in curved **talons**. Male and female eagles look similar, although the females are usually larger than the males. Eagles are related to hawks, falcons, and vultures.

Eagle

The word eagle comes from the Latin word "aquila," the name given to the golden eagle by the Romans.

fact

This large Verreaux's eagle has a wingspan of more than 6 ft (2 m). It swoops down on **prey** animals, which it catches as they run along the ground.

What's a bird?

Birds have a variety of features that make them different from other animals. Their bodies are covered in feathers and they have wings, rather than arms. Female birds lay eggs that hatch into chicks.

Eagles have a hooked beak for ripping flesh.

Eagle types

There are about sixty different species, or types, of eagles. Most eagles are larger and more powerful than other hunting birds, such as hawks. Eagles are divided into four groups: snake eagles, fish eagles, booted eagles, and giant forest eagles.

The bateleur eagle is a snake eagle. Its name comes from the French word meaning "acrobat."

The hawk eagle is a booted eagle. It has short, rounded wings and a rounded tail.

Four groups of eagles

Booted eagles get their name from their thickly feathered legs. Bald eagles belong to the fish and sea eagles group. They usually live near water and catch fish. Snake eagles are small and feed on snakes. The giant forest eagles are the largest and most powerful eagles and they live in tropical rainforests.

The greater spotted eagle is a booted eagle. It is about 28 in (70 cm) long from its head to its tail tip.

Vital Statistics

The great harpy eagle has a wingspan of up to 6½ ft (2 m) and the females may weigh as much as 20 lb (9 kg). One of the smallest eagles is the ornate hawk eagle, which has a wingspan of about 4 ft (1.2 m) and weighs less than 4½ lb (2 kg).

Where can you find eagles?

Eagles can fly long distances, so they are found in most parts of the world. However, they are not found in some of the more remote islands, such as New Zealand and Antarctica.

Bald eagles can be found in the far north of Alaska and Canada, where they have to survive long, cold winters.

All habitats

Eagles live in almost every kind of **habitat**, including deserts, coasts, and farmland. Bald eagles and golden eagles are found in the U.S.A. and Canada. Harpy eagles live in South American rain forests. The bateleur and martial eagles hunt over the savanna grasslands of southern Africa.

Some eagles have become used to people and have moved into towns and cities. Bald eagles even visit garbage dumps to look for food.

Eagle

Haast's eagle was the largest bird of prey ever. It weighed more than 45 lb (20 kg) and had a wingspan of 8½ ft (2.6 m). It once lived in New Zealand, where it preyed on another giant bird, the moa. Both Haast's eagle and the moa are now extinct.

fact

North America

Europe

Asia

Atlantic Ocean

Africa

Pacific Ocean

Pacific Ocean

South America

Indian Ocean

Australia

Antarctic Ocean

Antarctica

Areas where eagles are found today.

Building a nest

Eagles build huge nests in places that are difficult to reach, such as on ledges or high in trees. Eagle nests, also called **eyries**, are made from twigs. The inside is lined with soft grass or leaves.

Eagles return to the same nest every year, adding more twigs each time. Some old nests become so big and heavy that they break the supporting branches and crash to the ground.

Usually the male eagle collects the twigs and the female arranges them in the nest. It takes weeks, sometimes months, to build a nest.

A male bald eagle dives toward a female during a courtship display.

Courtship

Many eagles mate for life. This means that they live with the same partner until one dies. During their **courtship**, the male eagle brings the female gifts of food. Some males perform a courtship display, in which they dive toward the female from great heights or turn somersaults in the air.

Eagle

The largest known bald eagle nest was found in Florida. It was 9 ft (2.7 m) across, 20 ft (6 m) deep, and weighed more than 2 tons!

fact

Laying eggs

The female eagle lays between one and three eggs and sits on them to keep them warm. This is called **incubation**. The eggs hatch after about 60 days. The egg that was laid first is the first to hatch. The older chick is larger and grabs more of the food. Often, younger chicks die from starvation or are killed by the eldest chick. At least one of the chicks usually survives.

Young eagle chicks are covered in soft feathers and they can't fly.

After the chicks hatch, the female stays near the nest to guard them. The male brings them food.

Eagle enemies

Adult eagles have few enemies, but the chicks are often killed by snakes, raccoons, and other large birds.

Eagle

Young chicks are unable to control their body temperature. They depend on their mother to keep them warm and sheltered from the rain and sun.

fact

13

Growing up

Young eagles leave the nest when they are about one month old. They can't fly at this age, so they hop from the nest onto branches or ledges. Then they start to make short flapping jumps. Their jumps get longer and longer, and eventually the young eagles are able to make their first short flight.

Most adult eagles feed their young until they are between three and five months old. This gives young eagles plenty of time to practice flying and to learn how to hunt.

The young bald eagle on the right does not grow adult feathers until it is about three years old.

14

Young eagles have large wing and tail feathers to help them fly.

Eagle

Up to 90 percent of all eagle chicks die before they become adults. Some fall to their deaths and many others are killed by predators or die from starvation or disease.

fact

Changing feathers

Young eagles have different colored feathers from their parents. Often the young eagles have light and dark brown feathers on their back and paler feathers on their front.

Flying

Eagles are experts at flying. Their wings are long and wide, which helps them to glide. Many eagles can stay in the air for hours and hardly have to flap their wings at all.

A bald eagle flying in the air for an hour will flap its wings for as little as two minutes. This allows the eagle to fly long distances without using a lot of energy.

The eagle's wing feathers are separated at the tips. This helps air pass over the wing and makes the eagle's flight smoother.

A bald eagle dives at high speeds by folding back its wings. It opens them again to slow down.

Rising high

Eagles rise high into the sky using **thermals**. These are currents of warm air that rise up from the land. Eagles can fly over long distances using thermals. They are pushed up by one thermal, and then slowly glide down to catch the next thermal, which takes them back up again.

Eagle

The bald eagle is not really bald. It was named after the white feathers on its head and neck.

fact

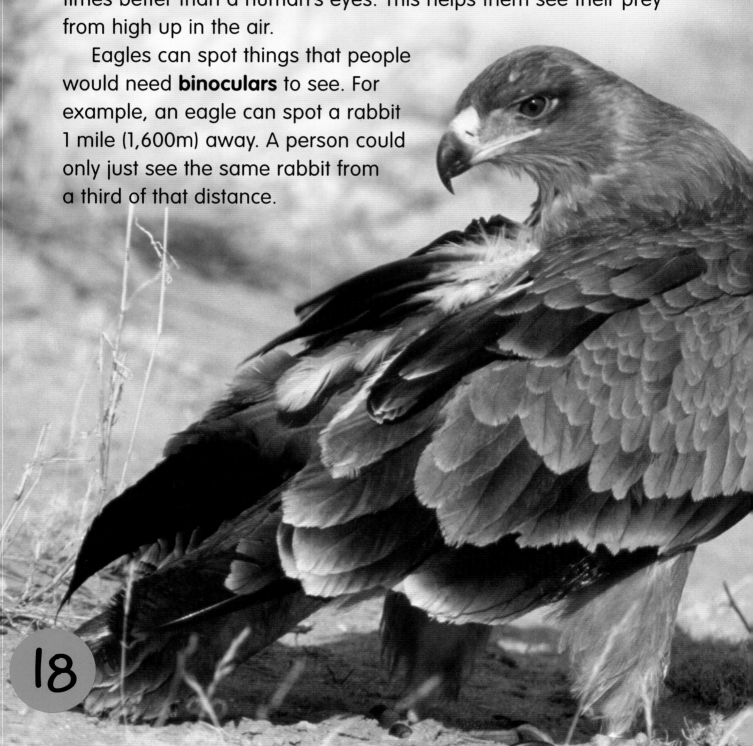

Eagle senses

Eagles have amazing eyesight. Their eyes can see at least four times better than a human's eyes. This helps them see their prey from high up in the air.

Eagles can spot things that people would need **binoculars** to see. For example, an eagle can spot a rabbit 1 mile (1,600m) away. A person could only just see the same rabbit from a third of that distance.

18

Hearing

Eagles have a well developed sense of hearing. They listen carefully for the noises made by their prey. However, their sense of smell is poor.

Eagles have a ridge over their eyes that makes them look very fierce, like this monkey-eating eagle.

Unlike human eyes, an eagle's eyes can't move from side to side. To look around, this eagle has to turn its whole head.

Eagle fact

If someone says you are eagle-eyed, it means that you see things far away that other people don't notice.

19

Feeding

Eagles are meat eaters. Most eagles feed on small mammals, such as rabbits and mice, or catch fish. However, snake eagles feed mostly on snakes and lizards. In South America, giant forest eagles, like the harpy, feed on a range of animals that live in the rain forest. They use their huge talons to catch monkeys, parrots, and lizards in the trees. The slow-moving sloth makes up one third of their diet.

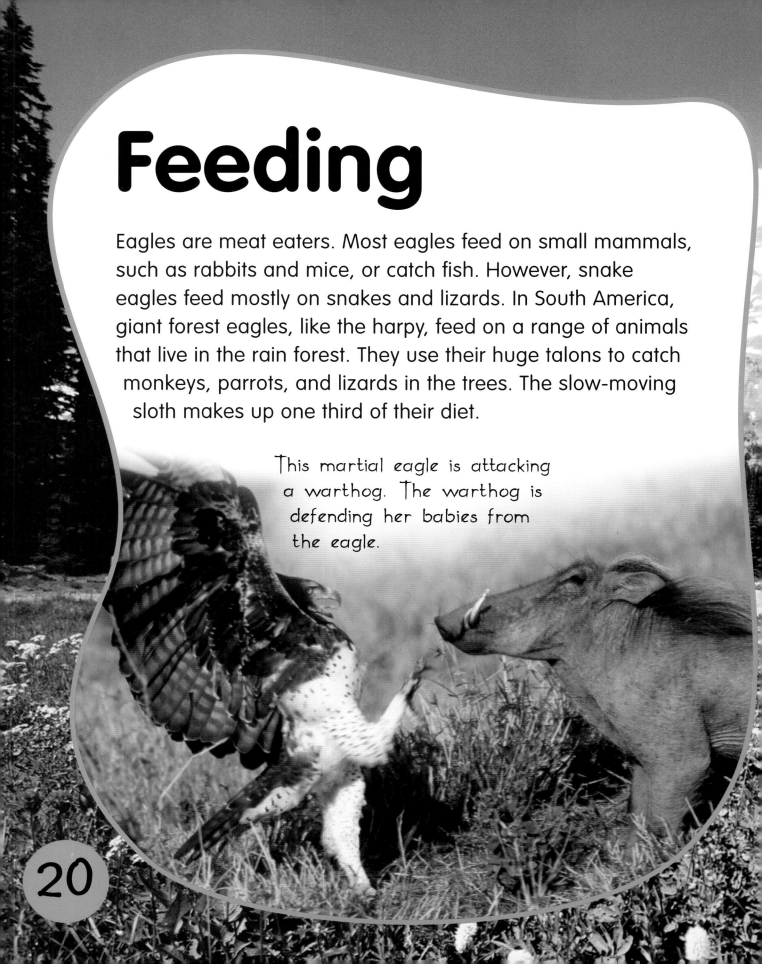

This martial eagle is attacking a warthog. The warthog is defending her babies from the eagle.

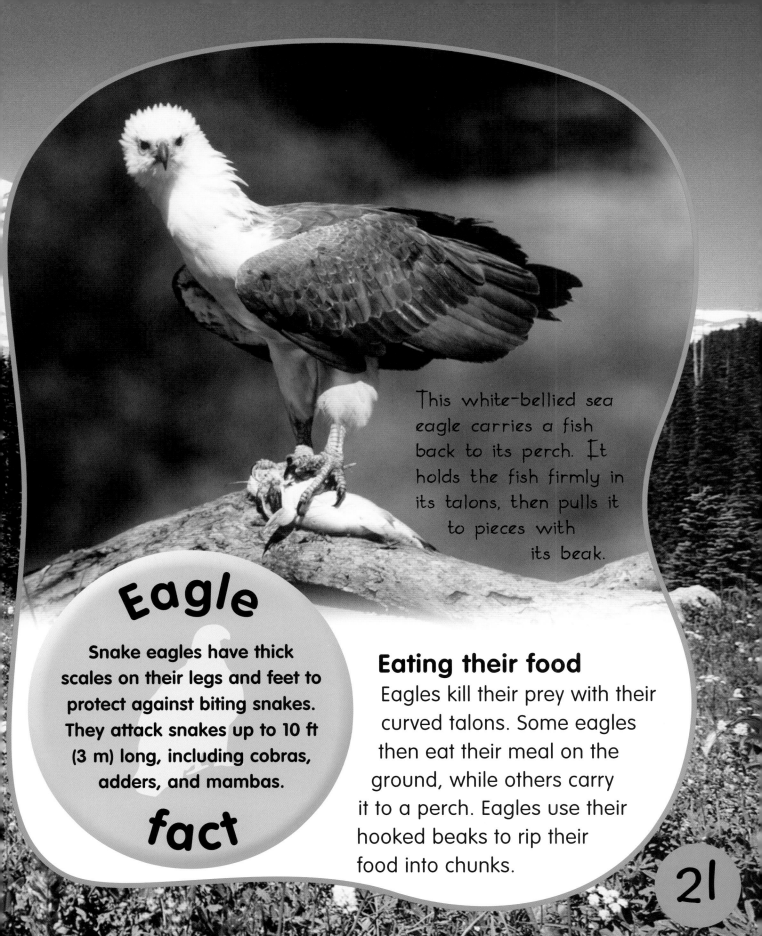

This white-bellied sea eagle carries a fish back to its perch. It holds the fish firmly in its talons, then pulls it to pieces with its beak.

Eagle

Snake eagles have thick scales on their legs and feet to protect against biting snakes. They attack snakes up to 10 ft (3 m) long, including cobras, adders, and mambas.

fact

Eating their food

Eagles kill their prey with their curved talons. Some eagles then eat their meal on the ground, while others carry it to a perch. Eagles use their hooked beaks to rip their food into chunks.

21

Hunting

Eagles hunt during the day so they can make the most of their excellent sight. Some eagles sit at the top of a tree or on a cliff ledge watching for prey. They stay perfectly still so their prey doesn't notice them. When it sees something, the eagle dives down and grabs it.

Eagle

The bateleur eagle spends most of the day in the air. It takes off as soon as the day warms up and flies almost continuously until the cooler evening hours. It can cover 185 miles (300 km) a day looking for food.

fact

This Steller's sea-eagle sees a fish in the water and is about to take off from its perch.

Searching from the air

Other eagles, such as the golden eagle, fly around looking for prey. When they see an animal, they swoop down and catch it in their talons. Forest eagles must steer between tree branches to catch their prey. Sea eagles are known as the pirates of the eagle world because they steal prey from other birds.

The eagle uses its powerful hooked talons to catch and carry prey.

The martial eagle is the largest eagle in Africa. It perches in trees in the early morning and evening. The rest of the time it spends in the air.

23

Territories

Most pairs of eagles live in a **territory**, an area where they find all of their food and make their nests. The size of a territory depends on the amount of food available and the size of the eagles. The biggest eagles generally occupy the largest territory. For example, a pair of golden eagles may live in an area about 60 square miles (100 sq km)—the size of a city.

Most golden eagles are found in mountainous areas, where they nest on rocky cliffs.

Fighting other eagles

Eagles defend their territory and chase away intruders. However, younger eagles may not have a territory, so they fly around, passing through the territories of older eagles. If one of a pair of eagles dies during the breeding season, a young eagle will move in and take the place of the dead bird.

Eagle

A group of several eagles soaring in a thermal together is described as a "kettle of eagles."

fact

This bald eagle is trying to chase away another adult bald eagle.

25

Eagle communication

Eagles communicate with each other using flight displays and calls. Some male eagles perform diving displays high above their territory to tell others nearby that the area is occupied.

Golden eagles are mostly silent, except during the breeding season. They use nine different calls to communicate.

Bald eagles have a screeching call similar to a seagull's.

Eagle calls

Eagles are normally quiet birds and they can't sing. But they do use calls to communicate with each other. The calls are shrill shrieks or high-pitched twitters. Some calls are warnings to other eagles, while other calls are used to attract attention.

Male and female eagles make calls to greet each other at their nest and to call to their chicks.

Eagle

The courtship of the bald eagle includes spectacular displays in which two birds grasp each other's feet high in the air and spin toward the ground, cartwheeling with their wings and legs outstretched.

fact

27

Eagles under threat

Eagles everywhere are in danger. The main threat comes from the loss of their **habitat**. For example, forests are being cleared for lumber and to make way for new farmland.

Large eagles prey on lambs, birds, and pigs, so in some countries farmers kill or **poison** eagles. However, the golden and bald eagles, and many others, are protected and it is illegal to harm them.

The giant forest eagle's habitat is destroyed when tropical rain forests are cut down.

Eagle conservation

One way to save the eagles is to **conserve** their habitat and their nesting sites, especially rain forests. Many countries have laws against killing eagles or collecting their eggs.

These people have traveled a long way to watch bald eagles in Homer, Alaska, in winter.

Eagle

Three species of eagle are likely to become extinct soon. They are the Madagascar serpent eagle, the Madagascar fish eagle, and the Philippine eagle.

fact

Life cycle

Eagles breed once a year. The female lays up to three eggs, which take 60 days to hatch. Young eagles leave their parents when they are about four months old. They begin to breed at between two and nine years of age. Eagles live up to thirty years in the wild and up to sixty years in captivity.

Chick in nest

Older chick leaving nest

Adult eagle

Glossary

binoculars a pair of tubes with lenses at either end that you look through to see things far away (often used by birdwatchers). The lenses make things looks bigger.

bird of prey a bird that hunts other animals for food

conserve to protect wildlife from being damaged or destroyed by the activities of humans

courtship an animal's behavior that attracts a mate

extinct no longer any left alive

eyrie an eagle's nest

habitat the place where an animal lives

incubation when something is kept warm

Latin an old language spoken by the Romans

poisoned killed or injured using a harmful substance

prey an animal that is hunted by other animals for food

talon the curved claw of a bird of prey, such as an eagle

territory an area where an eagle spends its life and where it finds all its food

thermal a current of warm air that rises into the air

wingspan the distance from the tip of one of a bird's wings to the tip of the other

Index

bald eagle 7, 8, 9, 11, 14, 17, 25, 27
bateleur eagle 6, 9, 22
beak 4, 5, 21
binoculars 18, 31
birds 5
birds of prey 4, 31
booted eagles 6, 7

calls 26, 27
chicks 5, 12–13, 14–15, 27, 30
communication 26–27
conservation 29, 31
courtship 11, 27, 31

displays 11, 26, 27

eggs 5, 12, 29, 30
extinct 9, 29, 31
eyesight 18, 19, 22
eyries 10, 31

feathers 5, 12, 14, 15, 16
feeding 14, 20–21
females 4, 5, 10, 11, 12, 13, 27
fighting 25
fish eagles 6, 7
flight 8, 14, 16–17, 22, 26
giant forest eagles 6, 7, 9, 20, 23, 28

golden eagle 4, 23, 24, 26
greater spotted eagle 7
growing up 14–15

Haast's eagle 9
habitats 9, 28, 29, 31
harpy eagle 7, 9, 20
hawk eagle 7
hearing 19
hunting 22–23

incubation 12, 31

kettle of eagles 25

Latin 4, 31
life cycle 30
life span 30

Madagascar fish eagle 29
Madagascar serpent eagle 29
males 4, 10, 11, 13, 26, 27
martial eagle 9, 23
mating for life 11
moa 9

nests 10–11

ornate hawk eagle 7

pairs (partners) 11, 24, 25
Philippine eagle 29
poison 28, 31
predators (enemies) 13, 15
prey 4, 21, 22–23, 28, 31

rain forest 7, 9, 20, 28, 29

sea eagles 6, 7, 9, 23
senses 18–19
size 7, 9
smell 19
snake eagles 6, 7, 20, 21
species 6
Steller's sea-eagle 22

talons 4, 20, 21, 23, 31
territory 24–25, 31
thermals 17, 25, 31
threats to eagles 28–29
types of eagles 6–7

Verreaux's eagle 4

white-bellied sea eagle 21
wings 5, 16
wingspan 4, 7, 9, 31